Zarathustra

FRIEDRICH NIETZSCHE

A Phoenix Paperback

This abridged edition published in 1996 by Phoenix
a division of Orion Books Ltd
Orion House, 5 Upper St Martin's Lane, London WC2H 9EA

This abridged edition reproduces selected extracts from the 1899 edition of
Thus Spake Zarathustra published by T. Fisher Unwin.

ISBN 1 85799 583 X

Typeset by Deltatype Ltd, Ellesmere Port, Cheshire
Printed in Great Britain by Clays Ltd, St Ives plc

Thus Spake Zarathustra: The First Part

ZARATHUSTRA'S PROLOGUE

I

Having attained the age of thirty, Zarathustra left his home and the lake of his home and went into the mountains. There he rejoiced in his spirit and his loneliness and, for ten years, did not grow weary of it. But at last his heart turned, – one morning he got up with the dawn, stepped into the presence of the Sun, and thus spake unto him:

'Thou great star! What would be thy happiness, were it not for those for whom thou shinest.

For ten years thou hast come up here to my cave. Thou wouldst have got sick of thy light and thy journey but for me, mine eagle, and my serpent.

But we waited for thee every morning and, receiving from thee thine abundance, blessed thee for it.

Behold! I am weary of my wisdom, like the bee that hath collected too much honey; I need hands reaching out for it.

I would fain grant and distribute until the wise among men could once more enjoy their folly, and the poor once more their riches.

For that end I must descend to the depth: as thou dost at even, when, sinking behind the sea, thou givest light to the lower regions, thou resplendent star!

I must, like thee, go down, as men say – men to whom I would descend.

Then bless me, thou impassive eye that canst look without envy even upon over-much happiness!

Bless the cup which is about to overflow so that the water golden-flowing out of it may carry everywhere the reflection of thy rapture.

Behold! This cup is about to empty itself again, and Zarathustra will once more become a man.'

Thus Zarathustra's going down began.

2

Zarathustra stepped down the mountains alone and met with nobody. But when he reached the woods, suddenly there stood in front of him an old man who had left his hermitage to seek roots in the forest. And thus the old man spake unto Zarathustra:

'No stranger to me is the wanderer: many years ago he passed here. Zarathustra was his name; but he hath changed.

Then thou carriedst thine ashes to the mountains: wilt thou to-day carry thy fire to the valleys? Dost thou not fear the incendiary's doom?

Yea, I know Zarathustra again. Pure is his eye, nor doth

any loathsomeness lurk about his mouth. Doth he not skip along like a dancer?

Changed is Zarathustra, a child Zarathustra became, awake is Zarathustra: what art thou going to do among those who sleep?

As in the sea thou livedst in loneliness, and wert borne by the sea. Alas! art thou now going to walk on the land? Alas, art thou going to drag thy body thyself?'

Zarathustra answered: 'I love men.'

'Why,' said the saint, 'did I go to the forest and desert? Was it not because I loved men greatly over-much?

Now I love God: men I love not. Man is a thing far too imperfect for me. Love of men would kill me.'

Zarathustra answered: 'What did I say of love! I am bringing gifts to men.'

'Do not give them anything,' said the saint. 'Rather take something from them and bear their burden along with them – that will serve them best: if it only serve thyself well!

And if thou art going to give them aught, give them no more than an alms, and let them beg even for that.'

'No,' said Zarathustra, 'I do not give alms. I am not poor enough for that.'

The saint laughed at Zarathustra and spake thus: 'Then see to it that they accept thy treasures! They are suspicious of hermits and do not believe that we are coming in order to give.

In their ears our steps sound too lonely through the streets. And just when during the night in their beds they hear a man going long before sunrise they sometimes ask: whither goeth that thief?

Go not to men, but tarry in the forest! Rather go to the animals! Why wilt thou not be like me, a bear among bears, a bird among birds?'

'And what doth the saint in the forest?' asked Zarathustra.

The saint answered: 'I make songs and sing them, and making songs I laugh, cry and hum: I praise God thus.

With singing, crying, laughing, and humming I praise that God who is my God. But what gift bringest thou to us?'

Having heard these words Zarathustra bowed to the saint and said: 'What could I give you! But let me off quickly, lest I take aught from you.' And thus they parted from each other, the old man and the man like two boys laughing.

When Zarathustra was alone, however, he spake thus unto his heart: 'Can it actually be possible! This old saint in his forest hath not yet heard aught of *God being dead*!'

3

Arriving at the next town which lieth nigh the forests, Zarathustra found there many folk gathered in the market; for a performance had been promised by a rope-dancer. And Zarathustra thus spake unto the folk:

'*I teach you beyond-man*. Man is a something that shall be surpassed. What have ye done to surpass him?

All beings hitherto have created something beyond themselves: and are ye going to be the ebb of this great tide and rather revert to the animal than surpass man?

What with man is the ape? A joke or a sore shame. Man shall be the same for beyond-man, a joke or a sore shame.

Ye have made your way from worm to man, and much within you is still worm. Once ye were apes, even now man is ape in a higher degree than any ape.

He who is the wisest among you is but a discord and hybrid of plant and ghost. But do I order you to become ghosts or plants?

Behold, I teach you beyond-man!

Beyond-man is the significance of earth. Your will shall say: beyond-man shall be the significance of earth.

I conjure you, my brethren, *remain faithful to earth* and do not believe those who speak unto you of superterrestrial hopes! Poisoners they are whether they know it or not.

Despisers of life they are, decaying and themselves poisoned, of whom earth is weary: begone with them!

Once the offence against God was the greatest offence, but God died, so that these offenders died also. Now the most terrible of things is to offend earth and rate the intestines of the inscrutable one higher than the significance of earth!

Once soul looked contemptuously upon body; that contempt then being the highest ideal: — soul wished the body meagre, hideous, starved. Thus soul thought it could escape body and earth.

Oh! that soul was itself meagre, hideous, starved: cruelty was the lust of that soul!

But ye also, my brethren, speak: what telleth your body of your soul? Is your soul not poverty and dirt and a miserable ease?

Verily, a muddy stream is man. One must be a sea to be able to receive a muddy stream without becoming unclean.

Behold, I teach you beyond-man: he is that sea, in him your great contempt can sink.

What is the greatest thing ye can experience? That is the hour of great contempt. The hour in which not only your happiness, but your reason and virtue as well turn loathsome.

The hour in which ye say: "What is my happiness worth! It is poverty and dirt and a miserable ease. But my happiness should itself justify existence!"

The hour in which ye say: "What is my reason worth! Longeth it for knowledge as a lion for its food? It is poverty and dirt and a miserable ease."

The hour in which ye say: "What is my virtue worth! It hath not yet lashed me into rage. How tired I am of my good and mine evil! All that is poverty and dirt and a miserable ease!"

The hour in which ye say: "What is my justice worth! I do not see that I am flame and fuel. But the just one is flame and fuel!"

The hour in which ye say: "What is my pity worth! Is pity not the cross to which he is being nailed who loveth men?

But my pity is no crucifixion."

Spake ye ever like that? Cried ye ever like that? Alas! I would that I had heard you cry like that!

Not your sin, your moderation crieth unto heaven, your miserliness in sin even crieth unto heaven!

Where is the lightning to lick you with its tongue? Where is that insanity with which ye ought to be inoculated?

Behold! I teach you beyond-man: he is that lightning, he is that insanity!'

Zarathustra having spoken thus, one of the folk shouted: 'We have heard enough of the rope-dancer; let us see him now!' And all the folk laughed at Zarathustra. The rope dancer, however, who thought he was meant by that word, started with his performance.

4

But Zarathustra looked at the folk and wondered. Then he spake thus:

'Man is a rope connecting animal and beyond-man, – a rope over a precipice.

Dangerous over, dangerous on-the-way, dangerous looking backward, dangerous shivering and making a stand.

What is great in man is that he is a bridge and not a goal: what can be loved in man is that he is a *transition* and a *destruction*.

I love those who do not know how to live unless in perishing, for they are those going beyond.

I love the great despisers because they are the great adorers, they are arrows of longing for the other shore.

I love those who do not seek behind the stars for a reason to perish and be sacrificed, but who sacrifice themselves to earth in order that earth may someday become beyond-man's.

I love him who liveth to perceive, and who is longing for perception in order that some day beyond-man may live. And thus he willeth his own destruction.

I love him who worketh and inventeth to build a house for beyond-man and make ready for him earth, animal, and plant; for thus he willeth his own destruction.

I love him who loveth his virtue: for virtue is will to destruction and an arrow of longing.

I love him who keepeth no drop of spirit for himself, but willeth to be entirely the spirit of his virtue: thus as a spirit crosseth he the bridge.

I love him who maketh his virtue his inclination and his fate: thus for the sake of his virtue he willeth to live longer and live no more.

I love him who yearneth not after too many virtues. One virtue is more than two because it is so much the more a knot on which to hang fate.

I love him whose soul wasteth itself, who neither wanteth thanks nor returneth aught: for he always giveth and seeketh nothing to keep of himself.

I love him who is ashamed when the dice are thrown in his favour and who then asketh: am I a cheat in playing? –

for he desireth to perish.

I love him who streweth golden words before his deeds and performeth still more than his promise: for he seeketh his own destruction.

I love him who justifieth the future ones and saveth the past ones: for he seeketh to perish on account of the present ones.

I love him who chastiseth his God because he loveth his God; for he must perish on account of the wrath of his God.

I love him whose soul is deep even when wounded and who can perish even on account of a small affair: for he gladly crosseth the bridge.

I love him whose soul is over-full so that he forgetteth himself and all things are within him: thus all things become his destruction.

I love him who is of a free spirit and of a free heart: thus his head is merely the intestine of his heart, but his heart driveth him to destruction.

I love all those who are like heavy drops falling one by one from the dark cloud lowering over men: they announce the coming of the lightning and perish in the announcing.

Behold, I am an announcer of the lightning and a heavy drop from the clouds: that lightning's name is *beyond-man*.'

5

Having spoken these words Zarathustra again looked at the folk and was silent. 'There they are standing,' he said unto his heart, 'there they are laughing: they do not understand me, I am not the mouth for these ears.

Must they needs have their ears beaten to pieces before they will learn to hear with their eyes? Must one rattle like a kettledrum and a fast-day preacher? Or do they only believe stammerers?

They have got something to be proud of. How name they what maketh them proud? Education they name it; it distinguishes them from the goat-herds.

Wherefore they like not to hear the word contempt used of themselves. Thus I am going to speak unto their pride.

Thus I am going to speak unto them of the most contemptible: that is of the *last man*.'

And thus Zarathustra spake unto the folk:

'It is time for man to mark out his goal. It is time for man to plant the germ of his highest hope.

His soil is still rich enough for that purpose. But one day that soil will be impoverished and tame, no high tree being any longer able to grow from it.

Alas! the time cometh when man will no longer throw the arrow of his longing beyond man and the string of his bow will have lost the cunning to whizz!

I tell you: one must have chaos within to enable one to give birth to a dancing star. I tell you: ye have still got chaos within.

Alas! the time cometh when man will no longer give birth to any star! Alas! There cometh the time of the most contemptible man who can no longer despise himself.

Behold! I show you the *last man*.

"What is love? What is creation? What is longing? What is star?" – Thus the last man asketh, blinking.

Then earth will have become small, and on it the last man will be hopping who maketh everything small. His kind is indestructible like the ground-flea; the last man liveth longest.

"We have invented happiness," – the last men say, blinking.

They have left the regions where it was hard to live, for one must have warmth. One still loveth his neighbour and rubbeth one's self on him; for warmth one must have.

To turn sick and to have suspicion are regarded as sinful. They walk wearily. A fool he who still stumbleth over stones or men.

A little poison now and then: that causeth pleasant dreams. And much poison at last for an easy death.

They still work, for work is an entertainment. But they are careful, lest the entertainment exhaust them.

They no longer grow poor and rich; it is too troublesome to do either. No herdsman and one flock! Each willeth the same, each is equal: he who feeleth otherwise voluntarily goeth into a lunatic asylum.

"Once all the world was lunatic" – the most refined say, blinking.

One is clever and knoweth whatever has happened, so that there is no end of mocking. They still quarrel, but they are soon reconciled – otherwise the stomach would turn.

One hath one's little lust for the day and one's little lust for the night: but one honoureth health.

"We have invented happiness," the last men say, blinking.'

And here ended Zarathustra's first speech which is also called 'the Prologue': for in that moment the shouting and merriment of the folk interrupted him. 'Give us that last man, o Zarathustra' – thus they bawled – 'make us that last man! We gladly renounce beyond-man!' And all the folk cheered smacking with the tongue. But Zarathustra sadly said unto his heart:

'They understand me not: I am not the mouth for these ears.

I suppose I lived too long in the mountains, listening too much to brooks and trees: now for them my speech is like that of goat-herds.

Unmoved is my soul and bright like the mountains in the morning. But they deem me cold and a mocker with terrible jokes.

And now they look at me and laugh: and while they laugh they hate me. There is ice in their laughter.'

6

Then a thing happened which silenced every mouth and fixed every eye. For in the meantime the rope-dancer had begun his performance: he had stepped out of the little door and walked along the rope that was stretched between two towers so that it hung over the market and the folk. When he was just midway the little door opened again and a gay-coloured fellow like a clown jumped out and walked with quick steps after the first. 'Go on, lame-leg,' his terrible voice shouted, 'go on, slow-step, smuggler, pale-face! That I may not tickle thee with my heel! What dost thou here between towers? Thy place is in the tower. Thou shouldst be imprisoned. Thou barrest the free course to one who is better than thou art!' – And with each word the clown drew nearer and nearer: but when he was just one step behind, the terrible thing happened which silenced every mouth and fixed every eye: uttering a cry like a devil, he jumped over him who was in his way. The latter seeing his rival conquer, lost his head and the rope; throwing down his stick he shot down quicker than it, like a whirl of arms and legs. The market and the folk were as the sea when the storm rusheth over it: everybody fled tumbling one over the other, and most there where the body was to strike the ground.

Zarathustra remained standing there, and the body fell down just beside him, badly disfigured and broken, but not dead. After a while, the consciousness of the fallen one coming back, he saw Zarathustra kneel beside him. 'What art thou doing there?' he asked at last, 'I knew it long ago that the devil would play me a trick. Now he draggeth me unto hell: art thou going to hinder him?'

'On my honour, friend,' Zarathustra answered, 'what thou speakest of doth not exist: there is no devil nor hell. Thy soul will be dead even sooner than thy body: hence-forward fear nothing.'

13

The man looked up suspiciously: 'If thou speakest truth,' he said, 'losing my life I lose nothing. Then I am not much more than an animal which by means of blows and tit-bits hath been taught to dance.'

'Not so,' Zarathustra said; 'thou hast made danger thy calling, there is nothing contemptible in that. Now thou diest of thy calling: therefore shall I bury thee with mine own hands.'

Zarathustra having said thus the dying one made no answer, but moved his hand as though he sought Zarathustra's to thank him . . .

OF THE DESPISERS OF BODY

'It is unto the despisers of body that I shall say my word. It is not to re-learn and re-teach what I wish them to do; I wish them to say farewell unto their own body – and be dumb.

"Body I am and soul" – thus the child speaketh. And why should one not speak like the children?

But he who is awake and knoweth saith: "Body I am throughout, and nothing besides; and soul is merely a word for a something in body."

Body is one great reason, a plurality with one sense, a war and a peace, a flock and a herdsman.

Also thy little reason, my brother, which thou callest "spirit" – it is a tool of thy body, a little tool and toy of thy great reason.

"I" thou sayest and art proud of that word. But the greater thing is – which thou wilt not believe – thy body and its great reason. It doth not say "I," but it doth "I" . . .

Behind thy thoughts and feelings, my brother, standeth a mighty lord, an unknown wise man – whose name is self. In thy body he dwelleth, thy body he is.

There is more reason in thy body than in thy best wisdom. And who can know why thy body needeth thy best wisdom?

Thy self laugheth at thine I and its prancings: "What are these boundings and flights of thought?" it saith unto itself. A round-about way to my purpose. I am the leading-string of the I and the suggester of its concepts.'

The self saith unto the I: "Feel pain here!" And there it suffereth and meditateth how to get rid of suffering – and that is why it *shall* think . . .'

OF READING AND WRITING

'Of all that is written I love only that which the writer wrote with his blood. Write with blood, and thou wilt learn that blood is spirit.

It is not easily possible to understand other people's blood. I hate the reading idlers.

He who knoweth the reader doth nothing more for the reader. Another century of readers – and spirit itself will stink.

That everybody is allowed to learn to read spoileth in the long run not only writing but thinking.

Once spirit was God, then it became man, and now it is becoming mob.

He who writeth in blood and apophthegms seeketh not to be read, but to be learnt by heart.

In the mountains the shortest way is from summit to summit: but for that thou needest long legs. Apophthegms shall be summits, and they who are spoken unto, great ones and tall.

The air rarified and pure, danger near, and the spirit full of a gay wickedness: these agree well together.

I desire to have goblins round me, for I am brave. Courage that dispelleth ghosts createth goblins for itself, – courage desireth to laugh.

I no longer feel as ye do: this cloud which I see beneath me, that blackness and heaviness at which I laugh, – that is your thunder-cloud.

Ye look upward when longing to be exalted. And I look downward because I am exalted.

Which of you can at the same time laugh and be exalted?

He who strideth across the highest mountains laugheth at all tragedies whether of the stage or of life . . .

I could believe only in God who would know how to dance.

And when I saw my devil, I found him earnest, thorough, deep, solemn: he was the spirit of gravity, – through him all
things fall.

Not through wrath but through laughter one slayeth. Arise! let us slay the spirit of gravity!

I learned to walk: now I let myself run. I learned to fly: now I need no pushing to move me from the spot.

Now I am light, now I fly, now I see myself beneath myself, now a God danceth through me.'

Thus spake Zarathustra.

OF THE NEW IDOL

'Somewhere there are still peoples and herds, but not with us, my brethren: with us there are states.

The state? What is that? Well! now open your ears, for now I deliver my sentence on the death of peoples.

The state is called the coldest of all cold monsters. And coldly it lieth; and this lie creepeth out of its mouth: "I, the state, am the people."

It is a lie! Creators they were who created the peoples and hung one belief and one love over them; thus they served life.

Destroyers they are who lay traps for many, calling them the state: they hung a sword and a hundred desires over them.

Wherever a people is left, it understandeth not the state but hateth it as the evil eye and a sin against customs and rights.

This sign I show unto you: every people speaketh its own tongue of good and evil – not understood by its neighbour.

Every people hath found out for itself its own language in customs and rights.

But the state is a liar in all tongues of good and evil: whatever it saith, it lieth; whatever it hath, it hath stolen.

False is everything in it; with stolen teeth it biteth, the biting one. False are even its intestines.

Confusion of languages of good and evil. This sign I show unto you as the sign of the state. Verily, this sign pointeth to the will unto death! Verily, it waveth hands unto the preachers of death!

Far too many are born: for the superfluous the state was invented.

Behold, behold, how it allureth them, the much-too-many! How it devoureth, cheweth, and masticateth them! . . .'

Of Chastity

'I love the forest. It is bad to live in towns: too many of the lustful are there.

Is it not better to fall into the hands of a murderer than into the dreams of a lustful woman?

And look at these men: their eye saith it – they know of nothing better on earth than to lie by a woman's side.

Mud is at the bottom of their soul; alas! if there is spirit in their mud!

Would ye were perfect, at least as animals are. But innocence is a necessary quality of animals.

Do I counsel you to slay your senses? I counsel the innocence of the senses.

Do I counsel chastity? Chastity is a virtue with some, but with most almost a vice.

True, these abstain: but the she-dog of sensuality looketh with envy out of all they do.

This beast and its no-peace followeth them even unto the heights of their virtues and into their cold spirit.

And with what grace the she-dog of sensuality knoweth how to beg for a piece of spirit, if it be denied a piece of flesh! . . .

Not when truth is dirty, but when it is shallow doth he who perceiveth dislike to step into its water.

Verily, they are some who are chaste to the bottom: they are more tender in their hearts, they like to laugh more and oftener than ye do.

They also laugh at chastity, asking: "What is chastity!

Is chastity not folly? But that folly hath come unto us, not we unto it.

We offered that guest house and heart: now he liveth with us, – let him stay as long as he liketh!" '

Thus spake Zarathustra.

OF LOVE FOR ONE'S NEIGHBOUR

Ye throng round your neighbour and have fine words for that. But I tell you, your love for your neighbour is your bad love for yourselves.

Ye flee from yourselves unto your neighbour and would fain make a virtue thereof; but I see through your 'unselfishness.'

The thou is older than the I; the thou hath been proclaimed holy, but the I not yet; man thus thrusteth himself upon his neighbour . . .

OF THE WAY OF A CREATOR

. . . Knowest thou, my brother, the word 'contempt?' And the agony it is for thy justice to be just unto those who despise thee?

Thou compellest many to relearn about thee; that is sternly set down unto thine account by them. Thy drawing near unto them and yet passing they will never pardon.

Thou goest beyond them: the higher thou risest, the smaller thou appearest unto the eye of envy. But he who flieth is hated the most.

'How could ye be just unto me!' thou hast to say – 'I choose your injustice as my portion.'

Injustice and dirt are thrown after the lonely one; but, my brother, if thou wouldst be a star, thou must shine unto them none the less!

Beware of the good and just! They would fain crucify those who invent their own standard of virtue, – they hate the lonely one.

Beware also of sacred simplicity! For it, nothing is sacred that is not simple; it liketh to play with the fire – of the stake.

And beware of the attacks of thy love! Too quickly the lonely one stretcheth out his hand unto him whom he meeteth.

Unto some folk thou shouldst not give thy hand, but only thy paw, and I would that thy paw might have claws . . .

Of Little Women Old and Young

. . . When I went on my way alone at the hour of sunset this day I met an old little woman who thus spake unto my soul:–

'Much hath Zarathustra said unto us women, but never hath he spoken unto us of women.'

And I answered her: 'Of woman one must speak unto men only.'

'Speak also unto me of woman,' she said; 'I am old enough to forget it at once.'

And I assenting thus spake unto the old little woman:

'Everything in woman is a riddle, and everything in woman hath one answer: its name is child-bearing.

Man is for woman a means: the end is always the child. But what is woman for man?

Two things are wanted by the true man: danger and play. Therefore he seeketh woman as the most dangerous toy.

Man shall be educated for war, and woman for the recreation of the warrior. Everything else is folly.

Over-sweet fruits – the warrior liketh not. Therefore he liketh woman; bitter is even the sweetest woman.

Woman understandeth children better than man doth; but man is more childlike than woman.

In the true man a child is hidden that seeketh to play. Up, ye women, reveal the child in man!

Let woman be a toy pure and delicate like a jewel, illuminated by the virtues of a world which hath not yet come.   Let a ray of starlight shine in your love! Let your hope be called: 'Would that I might give birth to beyond-man!' . . .

Then the little old woman answered me: 'Many fine things hath Zarathustra said, and especially for those who are young enough.

Strange it is, that Zarathustra little knoweth women, and yet is right regarding them! Is that because with woman nothing is impossible?

And now take as my thanks a little truth. For I am old enough for that.

Wrap it up and keep its mouth shut: Or it will bawl as loud as it can, that little truth.'

'Give me, woman, thy little truth,' I said, and thus spake the little old woman:

'Thou goest to women? Remember thy whip!'

Thus spake Zarathustra.

OF THE BITE OF THE ADDER

One day Zarathustra had fallen asleep under a fig-tree, it

was hot, and he had folded his arms over his face. Then an adder came and bit his neck so that Zarathustra cried out with pain. Taking his arm from his face he looked at the serpent: which recognising Zarathustra's eyes tried awkwardly to wriggle away. 'Not so,' said Zarathustra; 'thou hast not yet accepted my thanks! Thou wakedst me in due time, my way is long.' 'Thy way is short' said the adder sadly; 'my poison killeth.' Zarathustra smiled: 'When did ever a dragon die from a serpent's poison?' he said. 'But take back thy poison! Thou art not rich enough to make me a gift of it.' Then the adder again fell upon his neck and licked his wound.

Zarathustra once telling this unto his disciples they asked: 'And what, O Zarathustra, is the moral of thy tale?' Zarathustra thus answered:

'The destroyer of moral I am called by the good and just: my tale is immoral.

But if ye have an enemy return not good for evil: for that would make him ashamed. But prove that he hath done you a good turn.

And rather be angry than make him ashamed. And if ye be cursed I would have you not bless. Rather curse a little also!

And if a great wrong be done unto you straightway do five small ones in return! A horrible sight is he who is oppressed by having done wrong unrevenged.

Know ye that? Divided wrong is half right. And he who can bear it, is to take the wrong on himself!

A small revenge is more human than no revenge at all. And if punishment be not, at once, a right and an honour of the offender, I like not your punishing.

It is higher to own one's self wrong than to carry the point, especially if one be right. Only one must be rich enough for that.

I like not your cold justice; from the eye of your judges the executioner and his cold iron ever gaze.

Say, where is justice to be found which is love with seeing eyes?

Arise! invent that love which not only beareth all punishment, but all guilt as well!

Arise! invent that justice which acquitteth everybody except the judge!

Desire ye to hear this also? In him who wisheth to be just from the heart even a lie becometh a humanity.

But how could I be just from the heart? How could I give unto each what is his? Let this be enough for me: I give unto each what is mine.

Lastly, my brethren, beware of doing wrong unto any hermit! How could a hermit forget? How could he retaliate?

Like a deep well is a hermit. It is easy to throw a stone into it. But when it hath sunk unto the bottom who will get it out again?

Beware of offending a hermit. But if ye do, well, kill him also!'

24   Thus spake Zarathustra.

OF GIVING VIRTUE

. . . Zarathustra having spoken these words was silent like one who hath not yet uttered his last word; a long while he doubtfully balanced the stick in his hand. At last he spake thus, his voice having again changed:

'Alone I now go, my disciples! Ye go also, and alone. I would have it so.

Verily, I counsel you: depart from me and defend yourselves from Zarathustra! And better still: be ashamed of him. Perhaps he hath deceived you.

The man of perception must not only be able to love his enemies, but also to hate his friends.

One ill requiteth one's teacher by always remaining only his scholar. Why will ye not pluck at my wreath?

Ye revere me; but how if your reverence one day falleth down? Beware of being crushed to death by a statue!

Ye say ye believe in Zarathustra? But what is Zarathustra worth? Ye are my faithful ones; hence all belief is worth so little.

Now I ask you to lose me and find yourselves; not until all of you have disowned me, shall I return unto you . . .'

Thus Spake Zarathustra: The Second Part

OF THE PITIFUL

'. . . Would that my fate would always lead across my path such as are free from sorrow like you, and such as those with whom I *may* share hope and meal and honey.

Verily, now and then I did something for sufferers, but I always seemed unto myself to do something better when I learned how to enjoy myself better.

Since man came into existence he hath had too little joy. That alone, my brethren, is our original sin!

And when we learn how to have more joy we best get disaccustomed to cause pain and to invent pain unto others.

Therefore I wash my hand which helped the sufferer; therefore I even wipe my soul.

For on account of the sufferer's shame I was ashamed, when seeing him suffer; and when I helped him, I strongly offended his pride.

Great obligations do not make grateful but revengeful; and when a small benefit is not forgotten, it turneth into a gnawing worm.

"Be shy of accepting! Distinguish by accepting!" thus I

counsel those who have nothing to give away.

But I am a giver: willingly I give, as a friend unto friends. But strangers and paupers may themselves pluck the fruit from my tree: thus it causeth less shame.

Beggars should be abolished utterly! Verily, we are angry when giving them anything and are angry when not giving.

And likewise the sinners and bad consciences! Believe me, my friends: remorse of conscience teacheth to bite.

But the worst are petty thoughts. Verily, it is still better to act wickedly than to think pettily.

True ye say: "The pleasure derived from petty wickedness saveth us many a great wicked deed." But here folk should not try to save.

Like an ulcer is an evil deed: it itcheth and scratcheth and breaketh forth, – it speaketh honestly.

"Behold, I am disease" saith the evil deed: that is its honesty.

But the petty thought resembleth a fungus: it creepeth and cowereth and wisheth to be nowhere – until the whole body is rotten and withered with small fungi.

Unto him who is possessed by the devil I say this word into his ear: "It is better for thee to bring up thy devil. Even for thee there is a way unto greatness!"

Alas, my brethren! Of everybody one knoweth a little too much. And many a one becometh transparent for us; but for that reason we are by no means able to penetrate him . . .

One must keep fast one's heart. For if one letteth it go, how soon the head runneth away!

Alas! where in the world have greater follies happened than with the pitiful? And what in the world hath done more harm than the follies of the pitiful?

Woe unto all loving ones who do not possess an elevation which is above their pity!

Thus the devil once said unto me: "Even God hath his own hell: that is his love unto men."

And recently I heard the word said: "God is dead; he hath died of his pity for men."

Beware of pity: a heavy cloud will one day come *from it* for men. Verily, I understand about weather forecasts!

But remember this word also: All great love is lifted above all its pity, for it seeketh to create what it loveth!

"Myself I sacrifice unto my love, *and my neighbour as myself*," thus runneth the speech of all creators.

But all creators are hard.'

Thus spake Zarathustra.

The Night-Song

'Night it is: now talk louder all springing wells. And my soul is a springing well.

Night it is: only now all songs of the loving awake. And my soul is the song of a loving one.

Something never stilled, something never to be stilled is within me. It longeth to give forth sound. A longing for love is within me, that itself speaketh the language of love.

Light I am: would that I were night! But it is my loneliness, to be girded round by light.

Oh, that I were dark and like the night! How would I suck at the breasts of light!

And I would bless even you, ye small, sparkling stars and glow-worms on high – and be blessed by your gifts of light!

But in mine own light I live, back into myself I drink the flames that break forth from me.

I know not the happiness of the receiver. And often I dreamt that stealing was needs much sweeter than receiving.

It is my poverty that my hand never resteth from giving; it is mine envy that I see waiting eyes and the illuminated nights of longing.

Oh, unblessedness of all givers! Oh, obscuration of my sun! Oh, longing for longing! Oh, famished voracity in the midst of satisfaction!

They take things from me: but do I touch their soul? There is a gulf between giving and taking; and the smallest gulf is the most difficult to bridge over.

A hunger waxeth out of my beauty: I would cause pain unto those unto whom I bring light; I would fain bereave those I gave my gifts to. Thus am I hungry for wickedness.

Taking back my hand when another hand stretcheth out for it; hesitating like the waterfall that hesitateth when raging down – thus am I hungry for wickedness.

Such revenge is invented by mine abundance; such insidiousness springeth from my loneliness.

My happiness of giving died from giving; my virtue became weary of itself from its abundance! . . .'

OF SELF-OVERCOMING

. . . And this secret did life itself utter unto me: 'Behold,' it said, 'I am *whatever must surpass itself*.'

It is true, ye call it will unto procreation or impulse for the end, for the higher, the more remote, the more manifold; but all that is one thing and one secret.

I perish rather than renounce that one thing; and, verily, whatever there is perishing and falling of leaves, behold, life sacrificeth itself – for the sake of power!

That I must be war and becoming and end and the contradiction of the ends – alas, he who findeth out my will, probably findeth out also on what *crooked* ways he hath to walk!

Whatever I create and however I love it, soon afterwards I have to be an adversary unto it and unto my love. Thus willeth my will.

And ever thou, O perceiver, art but a path and footstep of my will. Verily, my will unto power walketh on the feet of thy will unto truth! . . .

Verily, I tell you: good and evil, which would be imperishable, – do not exist! Of themselves they must ever again surpass themselves.

With your values and words of good and evil ye exercise

power, ye valuing ones. And this is your hidden love and the shining, trembling, and overflowing of your soul.

But a stronger power waxeth out of your values, and a new overcoming. On it there break egg and eggshell.

And he who must be a creator in good and evil – verily, he must first be a destroyer, and break values into pieces.

Thus the highest evil is part of the highest goodness. But that is creative goodness.

Let us *speak* thereon, ye wisest men, however bad it be. To be silent is worse; all unuttered truths become poisonous.

And whatever will break on our truths, let it break! Many a house hath yet to be built!'

Thus spake Zarathustra.

OF SALVATION

When Zarathustra one day crossed the large bridge, cripples and beggars surrounded him, and a hunchback thus spake unto him:

'Behold, Zarathustra! Even the folk learn from thee and learn belief in thy teaching. But in order that they may believe thee entirely, one thing more is wanted – first thou must persuade us cripples! Here thou hast now a beautiful selection, and, verily, an opportunity with more than one forelock to catch it by. Thou mightest heal the blind and make the lame run, and thou mightest also perhaps take a little from him who hath too much behind him. That, I think, would be the proper way to make the cripples believe in Zarathustra!'

But Zarathustra replied thus unto him who had spoken: 'If one taketh the hunch from the hunchback, one taketh his spirit away. Thus the folk teach. And if one giveth the blind one his eyes, he seeth too many bad things on earth, so that he curseth him who hath healed him. But he who maketh the lame one run, hurteth him sorely; for just when he hath learnt to run, his vices run away with him. Thus the folk teach about cripples. And why should not Zarathustra learn from the folk, what the folk learn from Zarathustra? . . .'

THE STILL HOUR

'. . . Know ye the terror of him who falleth asleep?

Unto his very toes he is terrified by the ground giving way and the dream beginning.

This I tell you as a parable. Yesterday at the stillest hour, the ground gave way beneath me: the dream began.

The hand moved on, the clock of my life took breath. Nor did I hear such stillness round me. Thus my heart was terrified.

Then it was said unto me without a voice: "*Thou knowest it, Zarathustra?*"

And I yelled with terror at that whispering, and the blood went out of my face, but I was speechless . . .

Then it was again said unto me without a voice: "What

knowest thou *of that?* The dew falleth upon the grass when the night is most silent."

And I answered: "They mocked at me when I found and went mine own way. And in truth my feet trembled then."

And thus they spake unto me: "Thou unlearnedst the path; now thou also unlearnest walking!"

Then it was again said unto me without a voice: "What matter for their mocking? Thou art one who hath unlearnt obedience: now thou shalt command!

Knowest thou not who is required most by all? He who commandeth great things.

To do great things is hard; but to command great things is still harder.

This is what is most unpardonable in thee: thou hast the power and wantest not to rule."

And I answered: "I lack a lion's voice for commanding."

Then it was again said unto me like a whispering: "The stillest words bring the storm. Thoughts which come on doves' feet rule the world.

O Zarathustra, thou shalt go as a shadow of what must come. Thus thou wilt command and go in the front commanding."

And I answered: "I am ashamed."

Then it was again said unto me without a voice: "Thou hast still to become a child and without sense of shame.

The pride of youth is still upon thee; very late hast thou become young. And whoever wanteth to become a child must overcome even his youth."

And I meditated a long while and trembled. But at last I said what I had said first: "I wish not."

Then a laughter brake out around me. Alas, how the laughter tore mine intestines and ripped up my heart!

And it was said unto me for the last time: "O Zarathustra, thy fruits are ripe, but thou art not ripe for thy fruits!

Thus thou must again go into solitude; for thou shalt become mellow" . . .'

Thus Spake Zarathustra: The Third Part

THE WANDERER

. . . Now when thus mounting the hill Zarathustra thought on his way of his many lonely wanderings from his youth, and how many hills and mountain ridges and summits had been ascended by him.

'I am a wanderer and a mountain-climber,' said he unto his heart; 'I like not the plains, and it seemeth I cannot long sit still.

And whatever may become my fate and experience, – a wandering and a mountain-climbing will be part of it. In the end one experienceth nothing but one's self.

The time is past when accidents could happen unto me. And what *could* now fall unto my share that is not already mine own!

It merely returneth, it at last cometh home unto me – mine own self, and whatever of it hath been for a long time abroad and hath been dispersed among all things and accidents.

And one more thing I know: now I stand before my last summit and before that which hath been longest reserved for me. Alas, I must ascend my hardest path! Alas, I have begun my loneliest wandering!

But whoever is of my kin escapeth not such an hour, an hour which speaketh unto him: "It is only now that thou goest the way of thy greatness! Summit and precipice – these are now contained in one!

Thou goest the way of thy greatness. Now what was called hitherto thy last danger hath become thy last refuge!

Thou goest the way of thy greatness. Thy best courage must now be that behind thee there is no further path!

Thou goest the way of thy greatness. Hither no one shall steal after thee! Thy foot itself extinguished the path behind thee, and above it there standeth written: "Impossibility."

And if thou now lackest all ladders thou must know how to mount thine own head. Otherwise, how couldst thou ascend?

Thine own head, and past thine own heart! Now what is mildest in thee must become hardest.

Whoever hath spared himself always, at last aileth because of his sparing himself so much. Let that which maketh hard be praised. I do not praise the land where there – flow butter and honey!

In order to see *much* it is necessary to learn to forget one's self. This hardness is requisite for every mountain-climber.

But whoever is forward with his eyes as a perceiver, how could he see more than the foremost reasons of all things!

But thou, O Zarathustra, desiredst to see the ground and background of all things. Thus thou art compelled to mount

above thyself, up, upwards, until thou seest below thyself
even thy stars!

Ay, to look down unto one's self and even unto one's
stars: only that would I call my *summit*, that hath been
reserved for me as my *last* summit.' . . .

OF THE VISION AND THE RIDDLE

'. . . Then, suddenly, I heard a dog *howl* nigh unto the place.

Did I ever hear a dog howl like that? My thought went
back. Yea! When I was a child, in my remotest childhood.

Then I heard a dog howl like that. And I saw it as well,
with its hair bristled, its head turned upwards, trembling, in
the stillest midnight when even the dogs believe in ghosts –

So that I felt pity for it. For that very moment the full
moon in deadly silence passed the house; that very moment
she stood still, a round glow – still on the flat roof, as if she
stood on strange property.

Thereby the dog had been terrified; for dogs believe in
thieves and ghosts. And when I heard that howling again, I
felt pity once more.

. . . Between wild cliffs I stood suddenly, alone, lonely, in
the loneliest moonshine.

But there lay a man! And there! The dog, jumping, with
its hair bristled, whimpering – now it saw me come. Then it
howled again, then it *cried*. Did I ever hear a dog cry thus
for help.

And, verily, what I saw, the like I had never seen. A young shepherd I saw, writhing, choking, quivering, with his face distorted, from whose mouth a black heavy snake hung down.

Did I ever see so much loathing and pale horror in one face? Had he slept? Then the serpent crept into his throat – and clung there biting.

My hand tore at the serpent and tore – in vain! I was unable to tear the snake out of his throat. Then something in myself cried out: "Bite! Bite!

Off its head! Bite!" Thus something in myself cried out. My horror, my hate, my loathing, my pity, all my good and bad cried in one cry out of me . . .

But the shepherd bit, as my cry counselled him; and with a strong bite! Far away he spat the snake's head – and leaped up.

No longer a shepherd, no longer a man – a changed one, one surrounded by light who *laughed!* Never on earth hath a man laughed as *he* did.

O my brethren, I heard a laughter that was no man's laughter. And now a thirst gnaweth at me, a longing that is never stilled.

My longing for that laughter gnaweth at me. Oh, how can I endure still to live! And how could I endure to die now!'

Thus spake Zarathustra.

Before Sunrise

'. . . And "he who cannot bless shall *learn* how to curse!" – this clear doctrine fell unto me from the clear sky; this star standeth on my sky even in black nights.

But I am one who blesseth and saith Yea, if thou only art round me, thou pure! Thou bright! Thou abyss of light! Then I carry my Yea-saying with its blessing even into all abysses.

I have become one who blesseth and saith Yea. And for that purpose I struggled long and was a struggler, in order to get one day my hands free for blessing.

But this is my blessing: to stand above every thing as its own sky, as its round roof, its azure bell and eternal security. And blessed he who blesseth thus! . . .'

Of Virtue That Maketh Smaller

. . . 'I am Zarathustra the godless. Where find I my equal? And all those are my like who give themselves a will of their own and renounce all submission.

I am Zarathustra the godless. I have ever boiled every chance in *mine own* pot. And not until it hath been boiled properly, do I give it welcome as *my* meat."

And, verily, many a chance came unto me imperiously. But my *will* spake unto it still more so. Then the chance at once fell beseechingly upon its knees –

Beseeching to be given a home and heart with me, and persuading me flatteringly: "Behold, O Zarathustra, how ever friend cometh unto friend!"

But what say I where no one hath *mine* ears! And thus I will proclaim it into all winds:

Ye become ever smaller, ye small folk! Ye comfortable ones, ye crumble away! One day ye will perish.

From your many small virtues, from your many small omissions, from your much small submission!

Too much sparing, too much yielding – thus it is your soil! But for the purpose of growing *high* a tree will twist hard roots round hard rocks!' . . .

ON THE MOUNT OF OLIVES

. . . 'Whom I love, I love better in winter than in summer. Better I now mock at mine enemies, and more valiantly, now that the winter sitteth in my home.

Valiantly indeed, even when I creep into bed. Even then my hidden happiness laugheth and wantoneth; then laugheth my dream with its lies.

I, a – creeper! Never in my life have I crept before mighty ones. And if I ever lied, I lied from love. Therefore am I glad even in my wintry bed.

A poor bed warmeth me better than a rich bed; for I am jealous of my poverty. And in winter it is the most faithful unto me.

With a wickedness I begin every day: I mock at the winter by a cold bath. Therefore grumbleth my stern house-friend.

Besides I like to tickle him with a little wax-candle so that, at last, he may let the sky come out of ashen gray dawn.

For particularly wicked am I in the morning. At an early hour, when the pail clattereth at the well, and the horses with heat whinny through gray lanes –

Impatiently I wait, that, at last, the clear sky may open unto me, the wintry sky with its beard of snow, the old and white-headed man –

The winty sky, the silent, which often even keepeth its sun! . . .

How *could* they endure my happiness if I did not put round it accidents and winter sorrows and caps of polar bear-skin and covers of snowy skies!

If I had not pity for their *pity*, for the pity of these envious and malicious folk!

And if I did not sigh in their presence myself and chatter with cold and *allow* myself to be patiently wrapped in their pity!

This is the wise wantonness and good-will of my soul, that it *doth not hide* its winter and its snow storms; neither doth it hide its chilblains.

The loneliness of the one is the flight of the sick one; the loneliness of the other is the flight *from* the sick. . . .'

'. . . For the old Gods came unto an end long ago. And, verily, it was a good and joyful end of Gods!

They did not die lingering in the twilight, – although that lie is told! On the contrary, they once upon a time – *laughed* themselves unto death!

That came to pass when by a God himself the most ungodly word was uttered, the word: "There is one God! Thou shalt have no other Gods before me!"

An old grim beard of a God, a jealous one, forgot himself thus.

And then all Gods laughed and shook on their chairs and cried: "Is godliness not just that there are Gods, but no God?" '

Of Old and New Tables

10

'Thou shalt not rob!' 'Thou shalt not commit manslaughter!' Such words were once called holy; before them the folk bent their knees and heads and took off their shoes.

But I ask you: Where in the world have there ever been better robbers and murderers than such holy words?

Is there not in all life – robbing and manslaughter? And by calling such words holy, did they not *murder* truth itself?

Or was it a sermon of death, to call that holy which contradicted all life and counselled against it? O my brethren, break, break the old tables!

19

I draw around me circles and holy boundaries. Ever fewer mount with me ever higher mountains. I build a mountain chain out of ever holier mountains.

But whatever ye mount with me, O my brethren, see to it that no *parasite* mount with you!

Parasite – that is a worm, a creeping, bent one, that wisheth to fatten upon your hidden sores and wounds.

And *this* is its art, that it findeth out ascending souls, where they are weary. In your sorrow and bad mood, in your tender shame, he buildeth his loathsome nest.

Wherever the strong is weak, and the noble much-too-mild – there he buildeth his loathsome nest. The parasite dwelleth where the great one hath small hidden wounds . . .

20

O my brethren, say, am I cruel? But I say: 'What is falling already, shall be struck down.'

The All to-day – it falleth, it decayeth. Who would keep it? But I – I *will* strike down it besides!

Know ye the voluptuousness that rolleth stones into steep

depths? These men of to-day – look at them, how they roll into my depths!

A prelude I am of better players, O my brethren! An example! *Act* after mine example!

And him whom ye do not teach to fly, teach – how to *fall quicker!*

29

'Why so hard?' said once the charcoal unto the diamond, 'are we not near relations?'

Why so soft? O my brethren, thus I ask you. Are ye not – my brethren?

Why so soft, so unresisting, and yielding? Why is there so much disavowal and abnegation in your hearts? Why is there so little fate in your looks?

And if ye are unwilling to be fates, and inexorable, how could ye conquer with me someday?

And if your hardness would not glance, and cut, and chip into pieces – how could ye create with me someday?

For all creators are hard. And it must seem blessedness unto you to press your hand upon millenniums as upon wax –

Blessedness to write upon the will of millenniums as upon brass – harder than brass, nobler than brass. The noblest only is perfectly hard.

This new table, O my brethren, I put over you: 'Become hard!'

THE CONVALESCENT ONE

'. . . When the great man crieth, swiftly the small man runneth thither. And his tongue hangeth out of his throat from lustfulness. But he calleth it his "pity".

The small man, in particular the poet, – how eagerly doth he in words accuse life! Hearken unto him, but fail not to hear the lust which is contained in all that accusing!

Such accusers of life – they are overcome by life with a blinking of the eye. "Thou lovest me?" saith the impudent one. "Wait a little; I have no time yet for thee."

Man is the cruellest animal towards himself. And in all who call themselves "sinners" and "bearers of the cross" and "penitents," ye shall not fail to hear the lust contained in that complaining and accusing!

And myself? – will I thereby be the accuser of man? Alas, mine animals, that alone I have learnt hitherto, that the wickedest in man is necessary for the best in him –

That all that is wicked, is his best *power* and the hardest stone unto the highest creator; and that man must become better *and* more wicked.

Not unto *that* stake of torture was I fixed, that I know: man is wicked. But I cried, as no one hath ever cried:

"Alas, that his wickedest is so very small! Alas, that his best is so very small!"

The great loathing of man, – it choked me, it had crept into my throat; and what the fortune-teller foretold: "All is equal, nothing is worth while, knowledge choketh."

A long dawn limped in front of me, a sadness weary unto death, drunken from death, and speaking with a yawning mouth.

Eternally he recurreth, man, of whom thou weariest, the small man. Thus yawned my sadness and dragged its foot and could not fall asleep.

A cave became the human earth for me, its chest fell in, all that liveth became unto me mould of men and bones and a rotten past.

My sighing sat on all human graves and could no longer get up; my sighing and questioning cried like a toad, and choked, and gnawed, and complained by day and night:

"Alas, man recurreth eternally! The small man recurreth eternally!" . . .'

THE SEVEN SEALS
(OR THE SONG OF YEA AND AMEN)

I

'If I am a fortune-teller and full of that foretelling spirit that wandereth on a high mountain ridge between two seas, –

That wandereth between what is past and what is to come, as a heavy cloud, – an enemy unto sultry low lands and all that is weary and can neither die nor live –

Ready for the lightning in the dark bosom, and for the redeeming beam of light, charged with lightnings that say Yea! that laugh Yea! – ready for foretelling lightnings –

(But blessed is he who is thus charged! And, verily, a long time must he hang as a heavy thunderstorm on the mountain, he who shall one day kindle the light of the future!)

Oh! how could I fail to be eager for eternity, and for the marriage ring of rings, the ring of recurrence?

Never yet have I found the woman by whom I should have liked to have children, unless it be this woman I love. For I love thee, O Eternity!

For I love thee, O Eternity! . . .'

Thus Spake Zarathustra:
The Fourth and Last Part

THE HONEY-OFFERING

And again months and years passed over Zarathustra's soul, and he took no notice of it. But his hair grew white. One day, when he sat on a stone before his cave and silently gazed (there one looketh out on the sea and away over winding abysses) his animals went thoughtfully round him and at last stood in front of him.

'O Zarathustra,' they said, 'dost thou peradventure look out for thy happiness?' 'What is happiness worth?' he answered. 'For a long time I have not ceased to strive for my happiness; now I strive for my work.' 'O Zarathustra,' the animals said once more, 'Thou sayest so as one who hath more than enough of what is good. Dost thou not lie in a sky-blue lake of happiness?' 'Ye buffoons,' answered Zarathustra smiling, 'how well ye chose that simile! But ye also know that my happiness is heavy, and is not like a liquid wave of water. It presseth me, and will not part from me, and behaveth like melted pitch.'

Then the animals again went thoughtfully round him and once more stood in front of him. 'O Zarathustra,' they said, 'we see, it is *for that reason* that thou growest ever yellower and darker, though thy hair will soon look white and flaxy? Behold, thou sittest in thy pitch!' 'What say ye now, mine animals?' said Zarathustra laughing. 'Verily, I reviled when speaking of pitch. What I experience is experienced by all fruits which grow ripe. The *honey* in my veins thickeneth my blood and stilleth my soul also.' . . .

The Leech

And deliberately Zarathustra went further and deeper through forests and past moory vales. But, as cometh to pass with all who meditate on hard things, he stepped on a man unawares. And, behold, all at once a cry of pain and two curses and twenty evil abusive words splashed into his face, so that, in his terror, he lifted his stick and beat him on whom he had trodden. But immediately afterwards he recovered his senses, his heart laughing at the folly just done by him.

'Forgive,' said he unto the trodden one, who had got up *angrily* and sat down again. 'Forgive, and, above all, listen unto a parable.

As a wanderer who dreameth of distant things on a lonely road, striketh unawares against a sleeping dog, a dog which is lying in the sun;

As both of these, terrified unto death, start and snap at each other, like unto mortal enemies: thus it came to pass unto us.

And yet! And yet! How little was lacking for them to fondle each other, that dog and that lonely one! For both are lonely!' . . .

. . .'Who art thou?' he asked, and shook his hand. 'Between us many things remain to be cleared up and brightened. But already, methinketh, it becometh pure, broad daylight.'

'I am the *conscientious one of the spirit*,' answered he who had been asked, 'and in matters of the spirit, scarcely any one taketh things more severely, more narrowly, and harder than I, except thee from whom I learned it, Zarathustra himself.

Rather know nothing than know many things by halves! Rather be a fool on one's own account than a wise man on other folk's approbation! I examine things down unto the ground.

What matter whether it be great or small? Whether it be called swamp or sky? A hand's breadth of ground is enough for me; if it only be actually a ground and bottom!

A hand's breadth of ground – thereon one can stand. In the proper conscientiousness of knowledge there is nothing great and nothing small.'

But not long after Zarathustra had rid himself of the wizard, he again saw some one sitting by the way he went, namely a black tall man with a lean, pale face. *He* annoyed him sorely. 'Alas!' said he unto his heart, 'there sitteth affliction disguised. That seemeth unto me to be of the tribe of priests. What want *they* in my kingdom? . . .

'Whosoever thou art, thou wanderer,' he said, 'help one who hath gone astray, a seeker, an old man who may easily suffer injury here!

This world is strange and remote from me. Besides I heard wild beasts howl. And he who could have given me protection, liveth no more.

I was in search of the last pious man, a saint and hermit, who alone had not heard in his forest what all the world knoweth to-day.'

'*What* knoweth all the world to-day?' asked Zarathustra. 'Is it that the old God liveth no more, in whom all the world once believed?'

'Thou sayest it,' answered the old man sadly. 'And I served this old God until his last hour.

But now I am off duty, without a master, and yet neither free nor happy for a single hour, except in memory.

I have ascended these mountains, to arrange at last a festival for myself once more, as behoveth an old pope and church-father (for be it known unto thee: I am the last pope!) – a festival of pious memories and services.

But now even he is dead, the most pious man, that saint in the forest who constantly praised his God with singing and humming.

Himself I found no more when I found his hut. But I found two wolves therein which howled because of his death. For all animals loved him. Then I hasted away.

Had I come in vain into these forests and mountains? Then my heart resolved to seek another, the most pious of all those who believe not in God – to seek Zarathustra!' . . .

'Thou servedst him unto the very last' asked Zarathustra thoughtfully after a deep silence, 'thou knowest, *how* he died? Is it true what folk say, that he was suffocated by pity?

That he saw how *man* hung on the cross, and could not endure that his love unto man should become his hell and at last his death?'

But the old pope answered not, but gazed aside shyly and with sullen cheer.

'Let him go,' said Zarathustra after long meditation, still gazing straight into the old man's eye.

'Let him go, he is gone. And although it doth honour unto thee that thou speakest well of this dead one, thou knowest, as I do, *who* he was, and that he went strange ways.'

'Spoken under three eyes,' said the old pope cheerfully (for he was blind of an eye), 'in matters of God I am more enlightened than Zarathustra himself, and may well be so.

My love served him long years; my will followed all his will. And a good servant knoweth everything, and even many things which his master hideth from himself.

He was a hidden God, full of secrecy. Verily, even his son he begat not otherwise than by a secret way. At the door of belief in him standeth adultery.

Whoever praiseth him as a God of love, thinketh not highly enough of love itself. Did that God not also wish to be a judge? But the loving one loveth beyond reward and retaliation.

When he was young, that God from the East, he was hard and revengeful, and built up his hell for the delight of those he loved best.

But at last he grew old and soft and mellow and full of pity, more like a grandfather than a father, but most like a shaky old grandmother.

There he sat, withered, at his fireside, grieved because of his weak legs, weary of the world, weary of will, and one day suffocated by his all-too-great pity.' . . .

I love everything that gazeth brightly and speaketh honestly. But he – thou knowest well, thou old priest, there was something of thy tribe in him, of the priestly tribe. He had many meanings.

Besides, he was indistinct. How angry he was with us, this out-breather of wrath, because he thought we understood him ill. But why did he not speak more cleanly?

And if the fault was of our ears, why did he give us ears that heard badly? And if there was mud in our ears, go to! who had put it there?

In too many things he failed, this potter who had not served his apprenticeship! But in taking revenge on his pots and creations, for having turned out ill, he committed a sin against *good taste*.

There is good taste in piety also. And at last that good taste said: "Away with *such* a God! Rather have no God, rather be a fate for one's self, rather be a fool, rather be God one's self!" '

'What do I hear!' said then the old pope, pricking up his ears; 'O Zarathustra, thou art more pious than thou believest, with such an unbelief! Some God within thee hath converted thee unto ungodliness.

Is it not thy piety itself that letteth thee no longer believe in a God? And thine over-great honesty will one day lead thee even beyond good and evil! Lo, what hath been reserved for thee? Thou hast eyes and hand and mouth. They have been predestined from eternity for bestowing benedictions. One bestoweth benedictions not with the hand alone.

Although thou wouldst have thyself the ungodliest one, I perceive, when thou art nigh, a secret, holy, and goodly smell of long benedictions. From it I feel weal and woe.

Let me be thy guest, O Zarathustra, for a single night! Nowhere on earth do I now feel better than with thee!' . . .

OF HIGHER MAN

. . . Crookedly all good things draw nigh unto their goal. Like cats they arch their backs, they purr inside with their near happiness. All good things laugh.

The step betrayeth whether one walketh already on *his own* road. See me walk! But whoever draweth nigh unto his goal, danceth.

And, verily, I have not become a statue. Not yet I stand, benumbed, blunt, like a stone, as a pillar. I love quick running.

And although earth hath moors and thick affliction, he who hath light feet runneth even over mud, and danceth as on well-swept ice.

Raise your hearts, my brethren, high, higher! And forget not your legs! Raise also your legs, ye good dancers! Moreover it is better still if ye stand on your heads! . . .

The Sign

But the morning after that night, Zarathustra jumped up from his couch, girded his loins, and stepped out of his cave, glowing and strong, like a morning sun coming from dark mountains.

'Thou great star' he said, as he had said once, 'thou deep eye of happiness, what would be all thy happiness, if thou hadst not those for whom thou shinest!

And if they would remain in their chambers, while thou art awake and comest and givest and distributest, how angry would thy proud shame be at that!

Up! They sleep still, these higher men, whilst *I* am awake. *They* are not my proper companions! Not for them wait I here in my mountains.

Unto my work will I go, unto my day. But they understand not what are the signs of my morning. My step is for them not a call that awaketh them from sleep!

They sleep still in my cave. Their dream drinketh still at my drunken songs. The ear that hearkeneth for *me*, the *obeying* ear, is lacking in their limbs.'

This had Zarathustra said unto his heart, when the sun rose. Then he asking looked upward, for he heard above him the sharp cry of his eagle. 'Up!' he shouted upward, 'thus it pleaseth me and is due unto me. Mine animals are awake, for I am awake.

Mine eagle is awake and, like me, honoureth the sun. With an eagle's claws he graspeth for the new light. Ye are my proper animals. I love you.

But my proper men are still lacking unto me!'

Thus spake Zarathustra. Then it came to pass that he heard of a sudden that he was surrounded by numberless birds that swarmed and fluttered. But the whizzing of so many wings, and the thronging round his head were so great that he shut his eyes. And, verily, like a cloud something fell upon him, like a cloud of arrows discharged over a new enemy. But, behold, here it was a cloud of love, and it hovered over a new friend.

'What happeneth unto me?' Zarathustra thought in his astonished heart, and slowly sat down on the big stone which lay beside the exit of his cave. But while he grasped with his hands round himself, and above himself, and below himself, and kept back the tender birds, behold, something still stranger happened unto him. He unawares laid hold of dense warm shaggy hair. At the same time a roaring was heard before him, a gentle, long roaring of a lion.

'*The sign cometh*,' said Zarathustra, and his heart changed. And, in truth, when it grew light before him, there lay a yellow powerful animal at his feet, and clung with its head at his knees, and would not leave him, and did thus out of love, and did as a dog doth when he findeth his old master again. But the doves with their love were no less eager than the lion. And every time when a dove flew quickly across the nose of the lion, the lion shook its head and wondered and laughed.

Whilst all this went on, Zarathustra said but one thing: '*My children are nigh, my children*.' Then he became quite mute. But his heart was loosened, and from his eyes tears dropped and fell upon his hands. And he no more took notice of any thing and sat there unmoved, and without keeping the animals back any more. Then the doves flew to and fro and sat down on his shoulder, and fondled his white hair, and wearied not with tenderness and rejoicing. But the strong lion always licked the tears which fell down on Zarathustra's hands, and roared and hummed shyly. Thus did these animals.

This all took a long time or a short time. For, properly speaking, for such things there is *no* time on earth. But in the meantime the higher men had awakened in Zarathustra's cave and arranged themselves into a procession in order to go to meet Zarathustra and to offer him their morning greeting. For they had found, when they awoke, that he no more dwelt among them. But when they came unto the door of the cave, and the sound of their steps went before them, the lion, terribly startled, turned all at once away from Zarathustra, and leaped, wildly roaring, towards the cave. But the higher men, when they heard him roar, all cried out as with one mouth, and fled back and vanished in a moment.

But Zarathustra himself, stunned and strange, rose from his seat, looked round, stood there astonished, asked his heart, remembered, and was alone. 'What heard I?' he at last said slowly. 'What happened unto me this moment?'

And immediately his memory came back, and with one look he understood all that had happened between yesterday and to-day. 'Here is the stone,' he said, and stroked his beard. 'On *it* I sat yester-morning. And here the fortune-teller stepped unto me; and here for the first time I heard the cry I heard this moment, the great cry for help.

O ye higher men, of *your* need it was that yester-morning that old fortune-teller told me his tale.

Unto your need he tried to seduce me and tempt me. "O Zarathustra," he said unto me, "I come to seduce thee unto thy last sin."

Unto my last sin?' cried Zarathustra, and angrily laughed at his own word. '*What* hath been reserved for me as my last sin?'

And once more Zarathustra sank into himself and again sat down on the great stone and meditated. Suddenly he jumped up.

'*Pity! Pity for the higher man!*' he cried out, and his face turned into brass. 'Up! *That* hath had its time!

My woe and my pity, what matter? Do I seek for *happiness*? I seek for my *work*!

Up! the lion hath come. My children are nigh. Zarathustra hath ripened. Mine hour hath come!

This is *my* morning. *My* day beginneth! *Come up, then, come up, thou great noon!*'

Thus spake Zarathustra, and left his cave, glowing and strong, like a morning sun which cometh from dark mountains.

Phoenix 60p Paperbacks

History/Biography/Travel
The Empire of Rome A.D. 98–190 *Edward Gibbon*
The Prince *Machiavelli*
The Alan Clark Diaries: Thatcher's Fall *Alan Clark*
Churchill: Embattled Hero *Andrew Roberts*
The French Revolution *E.J. Hobsbawm*
Voyage Around the Horn *Joshua Slocum*
The Great Fire of London *Samuel Pepys*
Utopia *Thomas More*
The Holocaust *Paul Johnson*
Tolstoy and History *Isaiah Berlin*

Science and Philosophy
A Guide to Happiness *Epicurus*
Natural Selection *Charles Darwin*
Science, Mind & Cosmos *John Brockman, ed.*
Zarathustra *Friedrich Nietzsche*
God's Utility Function *Richard Dawkins*
Human Origins *Richard Leakey*
Sophie's World: The Greek Philosophers *Jostein Gaarder*
The Rights of Woman *Mary Wollstonecraft*
The Communist Manifesto *Karl Marx & Friedrich Engels*
Birds of Heaven *Ben Okri*

Fiction
Riot at Misri Mandi *Vikram Seth*
The Time Machine *H. G. Wells*
Love in the Night *F. Scott Fitzgerald*

The Murders in the Rue Morgue *Edgar Allan Poe*
The Necklace *Guy de Maupassant*
You Touched Me *D. H. Lawrence*
The Mabinogion *Anon*
Mowgli's Brothers *Rudyard Kipling*
Shancarrig *Maeve Binchy*
A Voyage to Lilliput *Jonathan Swift*

POETRY
Songs of Innocence and Experience *William Blake*
The Eve of Saint Agnes *John Keats*
High Waving Heather *The Brontes*
Sailing to Byzantium *W. B. Yeats*
I Sing the Body Electric *Walt Whitman*
The Ancient Mariner *Samuel Taylor Coleridge*
Intimations of Immortality *William Wordsworth*
Palgrave's Golden Treasury of Love Poems *Francis Palgrave*
Goblin Market *Christina Rossetti*
Fern Hill *Dylan Thomas*

LITERATURE OF PASSION
Don Juan *Lord Byron*
From Bed to Bed *Catullus*
Satyricon *Petronius*
Love Poems *John Donne*
Portrait of a Marriage *Nigel Nicolson*
The Ballad of Reading Gaol *Oscar Wilde*
Love Sonnets *William Shakespeare*
Fanny Hill *John Cleland*
The Sexual Labyrinth (for women) *Alina Reyes*
Close Encounters (for men) *Alina Reyes*